Benjamín Vicuña Mackenna

Chile

Benjamín Vicuña Mackenna

Chile

ISBN/EAN: 9783742863256

Manufactured in Europe, USA, Canada, Australia, Japa

Cover: Foto ©ninafisch / pixelio.de

Manufactured and distributed by brebook publishing software
(www.brebook.com)

Benjamín Vicuña Mackenna

Chile

CHILE.

The Republic of Chile, which during the last few years has justly attracted the attention of the world by its energy both in peace and in war, occupies the narrow strip of country lying along the southwestern part of South America, between the Andes Mountains and the Pacific Ocean. It extends from the Camarones River, in 19° 12′ 30″ south latitude, to Cape Horn, in latitude 55° 59′. Its boundaries, then, are the Andes on the east, the Pacific on the south and west, and the Camarones River on the north, separating it from Peru. The boundary treaty, made with the Argentine Republic October 22, 1881, terminated a long controversy concerning the dividing line between the two countries, and gave to Chile the greater part of Terre del Fuego Island and all the Straits of Magellan. The new boundary line takes Cape Virgin on the Atlantic (Dunguenes Point) for its starting point, running directly south to the ocean, and west to the summit of Mt. Aymon, thence along the northern shore of the Straits of Magellan to where it intercepts the 52d parallel of latitude in longitude 70° west. Thence the line follows the Summit of the Andes to the northern extremity of the two countries. The boundary lines between Chile and Bolivia and Peru have not yet been definitely settled by treaty. In June, 1882, the Chilean administration submitted to Congress a bill making the Camarones River the boundary, thus annexing the rich Peruvian Tarapaca, and all the sea-coast of Bolivia, which formerly extended from the 24th parallel north to the Loa River, which separated Bolivia from Peru.

4

A lower range of mountains, called the Cordilleras of the Coast, runs parallel with the loftier Andes, and walls in the great central plain, leaving only narrow passes for the rivers which descend from the Andes.

The area of Chile in 1879 was 229,304 square miles; but now, with the additional territory provisionally occupied and perhaps permanently annexed, it is about 300,000 square miles.

TOPOGRAPHY.

The narrow, fertile strip of land which forms the territory of this small but energetic nation, may be regarded as the skirt of the Andes, sloping rapidly towards the Pacific, and traversed by numerous rivers which fertilize it, and which, if not navigable on account of the swiftness of their currents, yet offer an invaluable motive force for all the modern industries which need for their propulsion a cheap power. The natural declivity of the country will produce, in a few hundred yards, fall enough for the largest wheels. The peculiarity of this territory, aside from the diversity of its climate, which varies from that of the tropics to that of the antarctic regions, is the variety of its geological and topographical structure, wrought out by the two great natural forces, the Cordilleras and the ocean.

The first or *northern section* or zone, which includes the old provinces of Atacama and Coquimbo to the Aconcagua River and the territories of Antofogasta and Tarapaca recently acquired, is composed for the most part of sterile lands covered with sea-sand, but prodigiously rich in minerals. This may be justly denominated the *mineral zone*. The province of Coquimbo alone produces one-fifth of all the copper consumed in the world. The province of Atacama has exported and is exporting as much silver as Potosi in Bolivia, Guanajuato in Mexico, and Nevada in the United States together; while Taltal, Antofogasta and Tarapaca are able to supply all the markets of the world with saltpetre, borax and gypsum. All the northern part of Chile is rich in minerals, and its scanty rivers have been abundant in gold.

The second zone which commences at the Aconcagua
River and extends to the Bio-Bio, called, on account of its
length, breadth and historic fame, "the King of Chilean
rivers," may be denominated the *agricultural section* or central
plain (*llano*). It is formed of a series of extensive, almost
level, valleys, which give every appearance of once having
served as basins for great lakes, whose waters, on retiring, left
rich deposits of soil brought down from the mountains,
and which to-day yield such abundant crops of cereals. In
these old sea-bottoms are found fossil remains of extinct
animals, relics of primitive man, and rare fragments of the age
of stone. This section includes the provinces of Valparaiso,
Aconcagua, Santiago, Colchagua, Talca, Maule, Nuble,
Linares and Concepcion. After passing the Maule, the central valleys do not have the same lake-basin form as those just
to the north.

The mean breadth of these valleys is from 75 to
100 miles, and counting from the Andes to the Pacific
it is from 150 to 180 miles. The total length of the territory
from the Camarones River to Cape Horn is a little over thirty-
six degrees, or nearly 2,500 miles.

The third zone, which extends from the Bio-Bio to the
Tolten River, has been occupied by the indomitable Araucanian Indians, who, to the number of thirty or forty thousand,
live as the Apachas of the north, without submitting to the
laws of civilization. Araucania forms the most beautiful and
fertile part of Chile. The white race is rapidly encroaching
on these fertile lands. The frontier line, which was formerly
at the Bio-Bio, has been carried to the Malleco, sixty miles
to the south, and an effort is being made to extend it to
the Imperial or Cautin River, which divides Araucania
in the centre. At the south an effort is making to
advance from Valdivia to the Tolten River, thus closing in
these unconquered tribes between this river and the Cautin.
In this way these savage tribes will be reduced to the extremity
of finally submitting to governmental control, or of escaping to
the *pampas* (plains) of the Argentine Republic, through the
narrow mountain passes which that country has already begun

to fortify. The destiny of the Araucanians is as certainly sealed as is that of the " red skins " of the United States.

The fourth zone of the orography and hydrography of Chile includes the system of lakes not yet drained by plutonic action, as were those at the north. Of these the Andina lake Villa Rica, the source of the Tolten River, is the most picturesque, and Lake Llanquihue, thirty miles in from the coast, is the largest. This zone includes all the southern end of Chile, and is likewise the section of the great primitive forests.

CLIMATE.

The climate of these sections has the same variety as their latitudes. In the deserts of Antofogasta and Atacama it never rains except at intervals of many years; at Coquimbo and Copiapo only four or five inches of rainfall during the year. In the central section the fall is about thirty inches, and in the lake region sixty to eighty inches. It is a common saying in Chiloe and Valdivia, as in Boston, that " it rains thirteen months in the year." In general the climate of Chile is mild, healthful, and delicious. No venomous insects are known, nor any ferocious animals; nor has the country ever been visited with cholera, yellow fever, black erysipelas, or any other contagious disease except small-pox. The ravages of this disease are due not to the climatic conditions of the country, but to the careless and filthy habits of the lower race of people, the inefficiency of the sanitary regulations and lack of energy on the part of the authorities. The House of Deputies has just rejected (July, 1882) a bill for obligatory vaccination, which had passed the Senate unanimously a month earlier.

If it were not for the constant drain caused by this disease among the lower classes, and the fearful mortality of children, which reaches the incredible proportion of seventy-five per cent. of the births, it is the common opinion that Chile would have a population of five or six millions; that is to say, double or treble its present number. When all its productive territory is inhabited, Chile will sustain a population of from sixteen to twenty million people.

The winter months are June, July, and August; the spring months, September, October, and November; the summer months, December, January, and February; and the autumn months, March, April, and May. In the central part of the country, where are situated Santiago, in the great mountain valley at the foot of the Andes, and at Valparaiso, the principal port, it seldom rains, except during the winter months. All the harvesting north of the Bio-Bio is done in the open air, as in Italy and California.

The mean temperature at Santiago and Valparaiso, in latitude 33°, corresponds to that of Naples,—that is, to 42° north latitude,—and is considered a little hotter (5°) in summer than that of Paris and London, and not so cold in winter by 9 degrees. The mean temperature in summer is 70° F., and in winter 52°, and for the year 61°. There is not a milder, more uniform climate in all the world than that of Chile. So little variation is there, that for weeks, and even months, at some ports on the coast, the thermometer marks no change whatever.

During the three and a half centuries of European occupation, the climate was more or less uniform, occasional exceptions occurring in the way of periods of drought, which continued from three to nine years, and were followed by as many years of rain. So severe were some of these, that the crops and herds were nearly all destroyed. The droughts recorded in the history of the country were from 1637 to 1640, 1705 to 1718, in 1725, 1743, and in 1771. This last was followed in 1783 by the greatest flood ever known, Santiago having been almost destroyed by it. In the present century, the year of least rain, as marked at Valparaiso, was 1863, when only 4.48 inches fell; and the year of the largest quantity of rain was 1868, when 35 inches fell. After this last period, there followed several years of comparative drought; but since 1877 there has been a rainy period again, which still continues. From January 1 to September 1 of the present year, 17 inches of rain have fallen in the central section; and, as a rare occurrence, there have been heavy rainfalls at Cobija and Tocopilla, north of the desert of Atacama, as also at Callao and Lima, in

Peru. It is worthy of note that, in all parts of the desert of Atacama, there are still marks of great floods of former times; and when, as in the present year, there are rains on these sands, they are quickly covered with bright flowers, and even succulent grasses.

On account of its geographical configuration, southern latitude, climate, products, and clear skies, it has frequently been designated "the Italy of South America;" but the climate and geographical structure of this country show a greater similarity to California. The Andes correspond to the Sierra Nevada Mountains; and the central valley, from the Mapocho to the Maule, to the valley of the Sacramento and San Joaquin, except that these last rivers are navigable. The coast range is found in both countries, and the intervening valleys produce the same cereals, fruits, flocks, and herds. Gold abounds also in Chile, and before the discovery of this metal in California the gold mines and washings of Chile held the same place in the money market of South America that those of California hold in North America.

The earthquakes have been supposed to exert an active influence on the climate of Chile. It has been observed that almost all of these disturbances have been followed immediately by copious rains.

EARTHQUAKES.

The heaviest earthquakes that have been known in Chile since the conquest, are the one of May 4, 1633, which destroyed Carelmapu in the south; the memorable one of May 13, 1647, which was felt generally throughout the country, and which completely destroyed the capital with the loss of life of nearly one-third of the population, then about twelve thousand. Those of July 8, 1730, and May 27, 1751, caused great tidal waves, and destroyed the ports of Valparaiso and Concepcion. So complete was the destruction of the latter city, that it was rebuilt on an entirely new site several miles inland.

In the present century, as if the violent action of creation had been calmed in these territories, which geologists regard as of comparatively modern formation, the earthquakes have

been only local, and scarcely merit the name. The most notable have been the one on November 29, 1822, which again
destroyed Valparaiso; the one on February 20, 1835, which
destroyed Concepcion in its new site. During the entire century, thus far, the casualties have not been, all told, a hundred,
while the earthquake of 1860 on the eastern slope of the
Andes completely destroyed the city of Mendoza, causing a
loss of twelve thousand lives; those on August 13, 1868, and
May 9, 1877, which devastated the coast of Peru, the tidal waves
reaching far into the interior, carrying with them heavy vessels,
as was done in the bay of Arica with Wateree, a corvette of
the United States. These were only slightly felt in the centre
of Chile. Whatever influence may be attributable to volcanoes, in earthquakes, it is evident from observation that in
Chile they affect them perceptibly, decreasing or wholly
destroying their violence.

THE ANDES AND THEIR VOLCANOES.

The Andes, of which the most southerly peak forms Cape
Horn, present in Chile an immense range, their course being
north and south. Their base has a uniform breadth of about
a hundred and fifty miles. The rivers rising in them run
almost parallel at right angles to the Pacific, and cut the
mountains with immense gorges and canons. The rainfall
on the eastern side is much less, because the Cordilleras inter-
cept the moisture borne in from the Pacific. The Andes of
Chile are a somewhat homogeneous mass, having a mean alti-
tude of eight thousand to ten thousand feet, but without the
little table lands, as represented by some travelers and geog-
raphers. On the contrary, it is only at the north that the
Andes divide into two arms and form the high table-land of
Bolivia, the Jauja and Cajamarca, in Peru; the Riobamba, in
Ecuador; and, lastly, the extended and beautiful plains of
Cundinamarca, in New Granada.

According to Pissis, not less than seventy volcanoes,
extinct and active, crown the range of the Chilean Andes from
Mt. Isluga, and the San Pedro volcano, in the newly acquired
territory, to Mt. Sarmiento at the extreme southern limit

of the Republic. The most noted peaks are the following: Mt. Aconcagua, 22,418 feet; its near neighbor, Mt. Tupungato, back of Santiago, but hid from view, 21,104 feet; Mt. Maipo and its twin, Mt. San Jose, 17,660 and 18,145 feet respectively. The latter has been in a state of activity since March 2, 1881; its two columns of smoke being visible from Santiago. Naturalists have called attention to the fact that this eruption, in a long extinct volcano of the Andes, corresponds to the day, with earthquakes, which caused great damage in the centre of Europe, especially in Valais, Switzerland, and Agran, Hungary. Mt. Peteroa has been one of the most violent. It experienced a frightful eruption December 3, 1762. To the south of the Maule River rise two volcanoes, Chillan and Antuco, 6,110 and 9,184 feet respectively, which flame up alternately. The former threw out immense quantities of earth and rock in 1861 and 1863. Mt. Villa Rica looms up over the plains of Araucania with its shining dome, 15,990 feet high. South of it, Mt. Calbuco, 7,380 feet, mirrors itself in the crystaline waters of Lake Llanquihue. Still south, Mt. Corcobado, 7,511 feet, rises like a great hump, and is visible from the seas of Chiloe.

LAKES.

In the geographical region which we have designated as the lake zone, many are found. Lake Llanquihue, triangular in form, twenty to thirty miles across, is the largest. Others are Lake Mallalanquen, or Villa Rica, twenty-four miles in circumference; Lake Rinigue, the source of the Valdivia River; and Lake Ranco, the source of the Bueno River. In the highlands of the Andes are found several small lakes called the Duck Lakes, from the wild birds that inhabit them. The most notable is Lake Mondaca, near the source of the Maule River. At the mouths of most of the larger rivers little salt lakes or seas are formed by the sands which are thrown up, making dangerous bars, as in the Bio-Bio, Maule, and Bueno Rivers. The picturesque little lake, Acubo, a few miles from Santiago, 12,530 feet above sea level, affords a glimpse of real Swiss scenery.

ISLANDS.

Besides Chiloe Island and its numerous archipelagoes, Guaytcca Island, covered with dense forests, and the group of islands which form Smith's Channel, Chile has at little distance from her coast a series of islands beginning at Mocha Island, and extending to Pascua Island, discovered by the pirate Davis in 1680. Juan Fernandez Island, four hundred miles west of Valparaiso, is the most celebrated, as the home of " Robinson Crusoe."

HOT SPRINGS, OR THERMAL WATERS.

All the territory of Chile, by virtue of its volcanic formation, according to the observation of Darwin and Fitz Roy, made in 1835, is particularly rich in mineral waters. Especially is this the case in the immediate vicinity of the Andes. There is scarcely a valley that has not iron alkaline and sulphur springs, with valuable medicinal properties. They are found especially valuable for diseases of the skin and blood (anæmia and chlorosis), the organs of digestion, chronic rheumatism, and gout. Eighteen miles to the north of the capital are the Colina Baths, which have been in the possession of the Dominican Friars since the last century. The Apoquindo Baths are a short distance to the east and the Cauquenes Baths, known from time immemorial, are sixty miles to the south, near the head-waters of the Cachapoal River, some miles off from the southern railroad. These springs have large bathing establishments. That at Cauquenes Springs will favorably compare with like establishments in Europe and the United States, and is visited by nearly every foreigner who comes to Chile. But the baths which enjoy the greatest reputation for their medicinal properties are the Hot Sulphur Springs of Chillan, situated at the foot of Mt. Chillan, already mentioned. On account of the snows, they are accessible only in the summer months, but give promise of being visited quite as much as the Cauquenes Baths. The hotel accommodations are sufficient for a couple of hundred guests. Still farther south, in the Indian territory, are other springs resorted to by the Indians themselves.

RIVERS.

The rivers of Chile are counted by the hundred, but those to the north of the Aconcogua scarcely merit the name, except for the abundance of auriferous sands along their course, and the fertility of their alluvial deposits, which are irrigated from their waters and sustain the populations that inhabit their narrow valleys. The chief rivers of the northern zone are the Copiapo, watering the valley and city of the same name ; the Huasco, the Coquimbo, on which, near the sea, is the picturesque city of Serena ; the Limari, the Choapa, and the Ligua. In the central zone, the most noted for the fertility of the deposits, which, like the Nile, they bring down from the mountains to renew the soil, are the Maipo, the Cachapoal, the Tingueririca, and the Teno.

From the Maule south the larger rivers are navigable, but only for small vessels, on account of the rapidity of the currents and the sand-bars closing their mouths. The Maule is navigable to Perales ; the Bio-Bio, to Concepcion ; the Valdivia, to Valdivia City, at whose wharves the ocean steamers call ; and the Bueno to Osorno in the neighborhood of the lakes. In January, 1882, four steamers began to ply as far up as this industrious and prosperous town. All the rivers have their course from east to west, except the Loncomilla, which runs northward, and after receiving the waters of several tributaries disembogues itself in the Maule. The Mapocho, after passing the city of Santiago, entirely disappears in the sands, and six miles farther to the west reappears with its waters augmented, and thence flows on a true river, and joins the Maipo at San Francisco del Monte. The Bio-Bio has the purest waters, holding in solution scarcely a vestige of organic material. The Maipo is the most rapid, and carries the greatest amount of sediment. The following table will give the locality and length of the principal rivers:

Names of River.	Province.	Miles.
Bio-Bio,	Concepcion,	222
Aconcagua,	Aconcagua,	180
Cautin, or Imperial,	Valdivia,	150
Maule,	Maule,	150
Cachapoal,	Santiago,	144
Itata,	Concepcion,	138
Mataquito,	Talca,	138
Rapel,	Colchagua,	120
Bueno,	Valdivia,	111
Valdivia or Callacalla,	Valdivia,	102
Coquimbo,	Coquimbo,	93
Cruces,	Valdivia,	93
Maipu,	Santiago,	90
Copiapo,	Atacama,	90
Huasco,	Atacama,	90
Ligua,	Aconcagua,	87
Tolten,	Valdivia,	87
Laja,	Concepcion,	84
Loncotoma,	Aconcagua,	84
Limari,	Coquimbo,	81
Mapocho,	Santiago,	78
Vergara,	Arauco,	78
Juncal,	Atacama,	72
Tabaleo,	Arauco,	66

The coast waters of Chile, as also the lakes, are abundant in fish. Especially is this true in the vicinity of Juan Fernandez Island, where the quantity is prodigious. But the rivers are very meagre in fish except trout and *pejerreyes*, a very delicious fish, known only in Chile. In 1866 an unsuccessful attempt was made to stock the rivers of Valdivia with salmon, and just now another attempt is now being made to stock the Bio Bio and the Maule.

POPULATION.

The population of Chile, according to the last census (1875), as given by Mr. Asta-Buruaga, without taking into account the 40,000 Indians, was 2,075,971. Classified by sex it is as follows :

Men,	.	. 1,033,974
Women,	. .	1,041,997

By civil state as follows:

	Males.*	Females.*
Unmarried,	725,389	690,469
Married,	278,013	276,948
Widowers,	30,572	
Widows,		74,580

By grade of instruction as follows:

	Males.*	Females.*
Able to read,	270,908	206,413
" " " and write,	244,985	176,162
Not able to read or write,	518,081	659,422

By nationalities as follows:

	Males.	Females.	Total.
Germans,	3,143	1,535	4,678
Argentines,	4,560	2,623	7,183
Spaniards,	1,102	121	1,223
French,	2,408	906	3,314
English,	3,459	808	4,267
Italians,	1,725	259	1,984
North Americans,	821	110	931
Peruvians,	470	361	831
From other South American countries,	470	209	679
From other European countries,	1,211	199	1,410
From Asiatic countries,	132	4	136
Total foreign born,	19,500	7,135	26,635
" native born,	1,014,474	1,034,862	2,049,336
Grand total,	1,033,974	1,041,997	2,075,971

In addition to the above the respective registers of births and deaths up to December 31, 1878, gave a surplus of 79,058, making the total 2,155,029. The registers for 1879 were as follows:

	Male.	Female.	Total.
Births,	45,318	44,195	89,513
Deaths,	30,861	30,247	61,108
Living,	14,457	13,948	28,405

* Children included.

Which would make the population January 1, 1880, 2,183,434. The following table, by the same author, gives the population on that date, distributed by provinces and classified by sex:

POPULATION JANUARY 1, 1880.

PROVINCES AND TERRITORIES.	Square Miles.	SEXES.		TOTAL.
		MALE.	FEMALE.	
Territory of Magellan from Lat. 47° to Cape Horn, .	57,761	746	505	1,251
Chiloe Islands and continent to Lat. 47, ...	38,507	34,341	35,482	69,823
Llanquihue, . .	7,810	27,718	25,782	53,500
Valdivia, .	7,521	17,669	16,689	34,358
Arauco, ...	8,085	29,550	26,469	56,019
Territory of Angol,	2,117	12,084	10,484	22,568
Bio-Bio, . .	4,146	41,808	38,807	80,617
Concepcion,	3,382	82,782	84,079	166,861
Nuble, .	3,362	67,380	67,459	134,847
Maule,	2,771	60,576	63,512	124,088
Linares,	3,298	65,738	63,397	129,135
Talca,	3,177	56,089	57,516	113,605
Curico, .	2,754	50,635	53,010	103,645
Colchagua, .	3,588	74,927	77,700	152,627
Santiago, .	7,323	188,574	198,537	387,081
Valparaiso, .	1,504	90,138	89,949	180,087
Aconcagua, .	5,886	65,230	68,698	133,928
Coquimbo, .	12,307	81,315	83,250	164,565
Atacama, . .	48,409	42,122	32,709	74,831
Total,	224,008	1,089,400	1,094,034	2,183,434

The annual increase of population being about 20,000, the total December, 31,1881, should have been 2,223,434, though the actual population is probably somewhat larger.

The total area between 24 and 44 degrees of latitude being
129,721 square miles, the medium density is 17.26 inhabitants
per square mile. This leaves out of the computation the dis-
trict of Punta Arenas, in the Magellan Straits. Allowance
should be made, however, for the losses in the recent war, and
the absence from home of more than twenty thousand
men. To supply this deficiency the government has appropriated the sum of $200,000 annually, to encourage foreign
immigration. A like attempt, some years earlier, proved very
fortunate in the German colonies of Valdivia, Llanquihue and
Osorno, but so far no practical results have come from the
present attempt.

According to a statement prepared from the census of
1875, for the Philadelphia Exposition of 1876, by Mr. M. G.
Carmona, the population of Chile is distributed as follows :

In cities and towns, 713,167 ; in rural districts, 1,355,257.
There are 41 cities, 78 corporate towns, 186 villages, 83 ham-
lets and 35 ports. There are 17 provinces, 60 departments,
682 sub-delegations, and 2,738 districts, not counting the colonies of Angol and Magellan. The following are the most
populous provinces, departments and cities :

Provinces.	Inhabit's.	Departm'ts.	Inhabit's.	Cities.	Inhabit's.
Santiago	362,712	Santiago	193,517	Santiago	148,284
Valparaiso	176,682	Valparaiso	100,926	Valparaiso	77,575
Coquimbo	157,463	Rancagua	97,126	Chillan	19,044
Concepcion	151,365	Chillan	95,941	Concepcion	18,277
Colchagua	146,889	Talca	90,588	Talca	17,452
Nuble	136,880	Caupolican	74,102	Serena	12,265
Aconcagua	132,799	SanFern'nde	72,787	Copiapo	11,484

The following are the populations of the principal cities of
the Republic, according to the best calculations : Santiago, the
capital, on the banks of the Mapocho, 180,000 ; Valparaiso, the
principal port, 110,000 ; Talca, 21,000 ; Concepcion, 20,000 ;
Serena, 14,000 ; Copiapo, 12,000 ; Iquique, 9,000 ; Antofogasta,
7,000. Two-thirds of the people live in the rural districts, and
for this reason the nation is sometimes spoken of as *El huaso
Chile*: that is, "A pastoral country." The newly acquired

territories are estimated to have something over 60,000 inhabitants, as follows: Antofogasta (Bolivian and foreign), 19,500; Tarapaca (Peruvian and foreign), 42,000.

The following table from the last census, for the year 1875, gives statistics of other conditions of the population.

PROVINCES.	Population.	Deaths.	Proportion of deaths to population.	Marriages	Proportion of marriages to population.	Births		
						Legitimate.	Illegitimate.	Total
Magellan Colony,	1,144	62	1 in 18	20	1 in 57	47	14	61
Chiloe,	64,556	1,134	1 " 57	496	1 " 130	2,162	418	2,580
Llanquihue,	48,492	916	1 " 53	415	1 " 117	1,577	367	1,944
Valdivia,	37,481	618	1 " 61	239	1 " 157	1,134	482	1,616
Arauco,	140,896	3,099	1 " 45	916	1 " 154	4,131	2,133	6,264
Concepcion,	151,565	3,991	1 " 38	1,564	1 " 96	5,288	2,704	7,992
Nuble,	136,860	3,868	1 " 35	1,372	1 " 107	4,306	1,570	5,876
Maule,	237,314	6,257	1 " 38	1,622	1 " 145	7,450	4,009	10,48
Talca,	110,359	3,588	1 " 31	1,116	1 " 99	4,543	995	5,5
Curico,	92,110	2,312	1 " 40	7 3	1 " 125	3,281	535	3,810
Colchagua,	146,829	3,944	1 " 37	1,343	1 " 109	6,014	1,014	7,00
Santiago,	362,212	11,188	1 " 32	1,603	1 " 101	14,087	2,661	16,740
Valparaiso,	176,682	6,504	1 " 27	1,426	1 " 124	6,326	1,6 3	7,9 4
Aconcagua,	132,799	3,042	1 " 40	766	1 " 173	3,374	1,272	4,6 1
Coquimbo,	157,463	3,962	1 " 40	979	1 " 161	3,508	1,765	5,3 7
Atacama,	71,304	4,447	1 " 16	338	1 " 211	1,693	1,164	2,3
Total,	2,068,424	55,897	1 in 37	16,670	1 in 124	68,616	21,755	90,371

PUBLIC HEALTH.

The sanitary conditions of a country that is bathed continually in its whole extent by ocean breezes, and which interposes high mountain barriers to contagions from other countries, and more than this, occupying the temperate, the healthiest of zones, and having abundant means of support and all natural resources of hygiene in country and city, cannot be other than the most healthful. The natural indolence of a large part of the people, the extreme poverty of the masses, the classes being as distinct as in England, and the lack of local precautions, neutralize to a great extent these natural blessings. The great mortality of nursing children and from the prevalence of small-pox give evidence of this. In Chile only the strongest constitutions attain to manhood and old age, hence there is a notable absence of invalids; and the extraordinary vigor and strength of her laborers, soldiers, and sailors, Lord Cochrane compared with the best of the world. The following table gives the mortality in the hospitals of the Republic in 1878, and affords an approximate idea of the diseases most prevalent among the people, omitting the two already mentioned :

	Men.	Women.	Total.
Consumption,	1,377	1,047	2,424
Rheumatism,	429		429
Dysentery,	396	366	772
Fevers,	263	322	585
Heart Disease,	168	161	329
Pneumonia,	153	206	359
Diphtheria,	143	310	453
Congestion of the Lungs,	108		108
Syphilis,	66	85	151

Small-pox, which, during the colonial days, destroyed annually a tenth part of the mixed races, and raged among the aborigines, has been on the increase since 1864. In 1872 it was very bad, and since then the number of deaths annually resulting from this disease is counted by the thousand. Most of the deaths are among the lower classes, or those who have not been vaccinated. As already stated, on account of false notions of individual liberty the bill for obligatory vaccination was rejected, a few months since, by the lower house of Congress. In the year already mentioned, the deaths by months were as follows: January, 5,333; February, 4,398; March, 4,228; April, 3,937; May, 4,423; June, 4,215; July, 4,613; August, 4,773; September, 4,767; October, 4,940; November, 4,749; December, 5,523. The largest number occurred in December, being 9.9 per cent.; and the smallest number in April, being 7.1 per cent.

RACES.

Chile, in distinction from Peru, Bolivia, and almost all the the other South American countries, has had the inestimable benefit of having a homogeneous and almost single race. Neither the African, the Sandwich Islander, nor the Chinaman, has ever become acclimated here. The climate is perhaps too cold for his warm nature. The stray specimens have soon disappeared, or retired to the seaboard. The population is composed of two classes: the white race of pure Spanish

blood, or a mixture of this and other European races, and the
Creole or native mixed race, having a third to a fourth of
Spanish blood. In the three and a half centuries this has
thoroughly permeated and altered the primitive and indigenous population. From this alliance of the Spaniards with the
Araucanians or Chilean Indians, known under thirty or forty
tribal names, from the *Changos* of Atacama, as to the *Cuicos*
of Osorno, have come the two million inhabitants who, to-day,
under the name of horsemen (*huasos*) in the country, and rag-
ged men (*rotos*) in the towns and cities, constitute the power,
the productive wealth, the energy, and the conquering armies
of this country.

With regard to the indigenous race, it may be said that it
has entirely disappeared north of the Bio-Bio River. At the
beginning of the century a few tribes, with only a few thousand
members, remained in the provinces of the north and centre.
It is only in the remote parts of the valleys of the Huasco
and Elqui rivers that the ethnologist is able to find any families, or even individuals, of the aborigines who inhabited the
valleys of this country, and had their nationalities and confed-
erations when the Spaniards arrived. The Araucanians,
properly so called, are divided into three tribes or comprehen-
sive families, namely, the Pehuenches, who inhabit the valleys
of the Andes and their pine groves (*pehuen*); the Llanistas,
who live in the central valleys or plains (*llanos*), and are the
most warlike; and the Costinos, who have their residence in
the Cordilleras of the coast and the transverse valleys. These
last have nearly all submitted to government supervision.

POLITICAL ORGANIZATION.

The Republic is divided into seventeen provinces, exclu-
sive of Araucania, whose political and military capital is Angol;
and the colony of Punta Arenas, situated on the Straits of
Magellan. Most of these provinces are separated from each
other by rivers or mountain chains, and nearly all extend from
the summit of the Andes to the coast, each one being divided
into two, three, or four, or even as many as six departments.
Coquimbo has six; Valdivia and Llanquihue only two; San-

tiago, the most densely populated province, has five, and Valparaiso four. There is at present a project before Congress to set off the department of Rancagua from the province of Santiago and make it a province, and also to re-divide Talca Province, and give it a new department on the coast. The departments are again divided into sub-delegations or townships, which are very numerous, there being in all nearly four hundred. These divisions correspond to the cantons in France as the departments correspond to the counties in England and the United States. The sub-delegations are again divided into districts, the smallest political divisions in the Republic.

GOVERNMENT AND ADMINISTRATION.

Notwithstanding its federal system, this Republic is intensely unified. This national cohesion is attributable in part to the nature of the territory. The political constitution of Chile resembles that of the United States, whose governmental organization was taken as a model by the legislators of South America. There are four entirely distinct powers of government: the executive, invested in a president; the legislative, invested in a National Congress composed of an upper and a lower house; the judicial, invested in the various judges of the courts; and the municipal.

The president is elected every five years by the people, and since 1871 is not eligible to re-election except after an interval of one term. He has five ministers or secretaries, and is supported by a Council of State composed of eleven members, five of whom are named by the President himself under certain regulations, and the other six are elected by Congress. They hold office for three years. The salary of the President is $18,000 a year. He has also the privilege of residing in the Treasury Building. The salary of the ministers is $6,000 a year. The members of the Council of State give their services gratuitously, and are of little consequence, because of the excessive power given to the President. The provinces are governed by *intendentes* named by the President, and removed at his will. Their salary is $4,000 a year with residence. The departments are presided over by Governors

named in the same way. There are three classes, according
to the salary, which varies from $1,000 to $2,500. The sub-
delegations are presided over by sub-delegates appointed by
the governors, and the districts by inspectors appointed by the
sub-delegates. These last two offices are without salary, and
hence do not greatly benefit the country.

The National Congress is composed of two houses, and
its members are elected every three years. The Senate has
thirty-seven members elected by the provinces, and the House
of Deputies one hundred and eight members elected by the
departments. They give their services gratis, and since 1876
the Deputies are elected by the system of cumulative votes
devised by John Stuart Mill. The judicial power is vested in
the Supreme Court, composed of six members, resident in
Santiago, who do not have any political functions. On the
contrary, in 1881 a law was passed establishing the incompati-
bility of the judicial and legislative functions. The Supreme
Court is occupied chiefly with cases of real estate, war claims,
and criminal cases. Ordinary cases are tried before justices of
the peace (one in each department). There are also four courts
of appeal, sitting in Serena, Santiago (2), and Concepcion. In
Santiago and other thickly populated departments, there are
two, four, or even six, justices of the peace, civil and criminal.
Minor cases are very arbitrarily tried by sub-delegate justices,
who certainly are no benefit to the country.

Chile is fortunate in possessing an excellent codification
of her laws. The civil code was promulgated in 1858, and
the commercial code, penal code, code of mines, code of
organization of tribunals, etc., followed in order. The civil
code is taken largely from the code of Napoleon, and the
military code from the ordinances of Spain. The Republic
needs a naval code, but for the present the naval ordinances of
the mother country serve well.

The municipal authority is vested in city councils elected
every three years by the people, but their authority is so small
that they cannot appropriate more than a hundred dollars of
their incomes without the consent of the president of the
country. The receipts of the municipalities from licenses,

public lighting, and police taxes, and all other sources, were, in 1878, $4,500,404, and the expenses as follows:

Street cleaning and sanitary measures,	$416,515.69
Police,	741,428.99
Public works,	81,350.52
Public schools,	66,847.54
Benevolent institutions and prisons,	182,147.73
City government,	294,892.89
Interest and reduction of city debts,	2,555,513.35
Extraordinary and miscellaneous expenses,	164,709.63

Recently (1882) a rural police has been organized throughout the Republic, sustained by a small property tax. This important service, just now being tried, is in charge of a commission of land owners and contributors.

RELIGIOUS ADMINISTRATION.

In Chile there does not exist a separation of Church and State. The religion of the country is Roman Catholic, but Protestantism is tolerated, and in Valparaiso and Santiago there are Protestant congregations having chapels and supporting their own pastors. The State Church has one archbishop, nominated by the President and confirmed by the Pope. The archbishop resides at Santiago, and the bishops have their dioceses at Serena, Concepcion, and Chiloe. The State assists to maintain the Church in return for the tithes of the fruits of the land, which formerly it enjoyed, but of which it has been deprived. The archbishop and bishops receive salaries of $6,000 a year, and it is calculated the other revenues of the Church amounted, in 1881, to $237.030. The tithes appropriated by the State, since 1850, amount to five times this amount. At present, in consequence of disputes regarding the naming of bishops and archbishop, there is a strong feeling in favor of the separation of Church and State, in accordance with the principles of Cavour and the system in practice in the United States. The clergy of Chile are educated and moral, but insufficient, although there exists a fine theological seminary in Santiago, and five others at Valparaiso, Serena, Concepcion and Ancud. The whole number of native priests is not over four hundred, hence many come from Spain and Italy, and lend their services as curates and vice-curates. The number of students in the diocesan seminaries, in 1881, was as follows:

Seminary in Ancud,		32
"	Concepcion,	118
"	Santiago,	488
"	Serena,	87
	Total,	725

PUBLIC EDUCATION.

Public education in Chile is comparatively meagre, but in its higher courses is as thorough and finished as any in Europe. Unfortunately, however, the school system does not adequately provide for the practical and vital exigencies of the country. It has scarcely recovered from its Spanish origin, and possesses a strong French tendency, which has influenced its literature, tastes and industry. Fortunately the excess of evil has produced a reaction, and the youth are changing from a preference to the law which threatened to overrun the country to the more practical professions, as medicine, agriculture, civil and mining engineering, mechanics, etc.

Public education, as in France, is divided into three grades, superior, intermediate and primary. Santiago is the seat of the National University, which has five faculties and a council of higher public education, which superintends the higher and intermediate schools of the country. These schools are free, and have their own buildings, apparatus, etc. The principal one is in Santiago, founded in 1813, and called the National Institute. In the provinces these schools take the name of *liceos* or high schools. The University preparatory course in the National Institute in 1880 had 843 students, distributed as follows :—

Physical Science and Mathematics,	34
Medicine,	263
Law (nearly one-half),	389
Pharmacy,	86
Fine Arts (Drawing, Painting and Sculpture),	71

At the examinations in March, 1881, the following number were approved :

Science and Mathematics,	231
Medicine and Pharmacy,	874
Law,	975

In the intermediate course in the Institute there were 918 students enrolled, 128 being boarders and 790 day scholars. The high schools in the provinces made the following showing for the same year :

	Students.	Examinations.
Copiapo,	181	443
Serena,	220	560
San Felipe,	229	249
Valparaiso,	286	
Rancagua,	100	121
San Fernando,	35	
Curico,	101	196
Talca,	230	448
Linares,	64	67
Cauquenes,	76	113
Chillan,	146	361
Concepcion,	160	530
Los Angeles,	78	100
Lebu,	60	
Valdivia,	46	204
Puerto Montt,	51	102
Ancud,	93	
	2,176	

The intermediate and superior school instruction, under the maintenance of the State, has increased to nearly four

thousand students; but this is certainly much less than the
intellectual progress of the country demands. These ar
distributed as follows:

Superior course in the Institute,	843
Intermediate course in the Institute,	918
Intermediate course in the Provinces,	2,176
Total,	3,937

Fortunately, there exist in the capital special schools for
teachers, agriculture, and manual trades. There is also a
military academy, an academy of painting, a conservatory of
music, and in Valparaiso a naval academy, in all of which the
number of students maintained by the State is about five thousand, including the theological seminaries. In the private
schools there are, perhaps, as many more.

Primary instruction, which some time back received considerable attention, especially under the energetic administration
of President Montt (1851–61), is now somewhat neglected
by the State. Benevolent societies supply, in part, this deficiency. The whole number of scholars in all the schools of
the Republic in 1881 amounted to from sixty to sixty-five
thousand. The free public schools in operation in 1880–81
were as follows:

City schools, for boys,	114		
" " " girls,	141		
		255	
Country schools, for boys,	101		
" " " girls,	264		
		365	
			620
Established in 1881,			18
Total,			638

The number of children enrolled in all the public schools
in 1880 was 48,794.—24,961 boys and 23,833 girls. The
average attendance was 34,089. To this must be added the
private and society schools, which numbered 405, with 15,106

scholars,—9,218 boys and 5,888 girls. The total number of public and private schools open this year was 1,043, with an average enrollment of 64 scholars.

The public school expenses, in all grades, were the following:

National Institute, University Preparatory,	$56,841
" " Intermediate,	116,784
Provincial high schools,	208,777
Normal schools,	43,872
Primary "	385,377
Publication of text-books,	30,000
Administration, premiums, etc.,	106,195
Total,	$947,846

The total appropriation made by Congress for school purposes in 1881 was $1,119,620, and in 1882, $1,386,022. In Santiago is the National Library, with more than sixty thousand volumes. Just now it is being removed to a new edifice, and arranged according to the latest system. The University, Institute, and many private schools, as well as the provincial high schools, have excellent libraries also. In Santiago and Valparaiso there are museums of natural history; in Serena and Copiapo, museums of mineralogy; and a taste for the fine arts may be cultivated in the many private galleries of paintings, some of which are valued as high as twenty, forty, fifty, and even a hundred thousand dollars. In Santiago there are fifteen public statues, mostly of the great men of the revolution, as O'Higgins, Carrera, San Martin, Freire, Bello, etc. Valparaiso has erected monuments to Lord Cochrane and William Wheelwright, the introducer of steam navigation; and others of Admiral Blanco, Encalada, and the hero of Iquique, Arturo Prat, are being erected.

THE PRESS.

Printing was introduced in 1812, with a little screw-press brought from the United States, still preserved as a relic in the National Museum. Great advances have been made of late, especially under the liberal governments, which have granted the widest liberty to the press. In 1853 there was in Santiago only one daily, the *Mensajero*, and the *Araucano*,—the official organ. In 1855 the *Ferrocarril* was founded, and to-day it has a circulation of eight thousand to nine thousand copies, its profits being from twenty-five to thirty thousand dollars. In the last ten years there have been founded in nearly all the capitals of the provinces or departments, dailies and other periodicals; and some of the larger cities, as Iquique, Copiapo, and Serena, have as many as three dailies. In Valparaiso there are two large dailies : the *Mercurio*, the oldest, founded in 1827. This has the largest circulation. It prints from eleven to twelve thousand copies daily, and yields a net income of nearly forty thousand dollars. There is also an English weekly, *The Chilian Times*, and a German weekly. The dailies of Santiago are the *Ferrocarril*, the *Independiente*, the *Estandarte Catolico*, and the *Epoca*. The *Araucano*, the organ of the government, was converted into the *Diario Oficial* in 1877.

BENEVOLENT INSTITUTIONS.

The Chileans have ever been noted for their charitable and hospitable spirit. Pedro Valdivia founded in Santiago the first hospital. In all the larger cities there are now hospitals under the care of the Sisters of St. Vincent de Paul. These are aided by the State, and have also revenues of their own, from legacies, gifts, etc. In Santiago there are orphan, widow, blind, invalid, and lunatic asylums; the last having five hundred inmates. In 1873 there were treated in the hospitals and dispensaries of the Republic, 296,879 cases. All the cities have cemeteries; those of Santiago and Valparaiso rivaling in beauty and elegance the most magnificent of Europe. The hospitals are mostly under the charge of the Sisters of St. Vincent de Paul, who have their central convent in Santiago. The orphan and widow asylums are generally in charge of the Sisters of the Providencia, from Canada. Since 1853 they have founded six convents in Santiago, Valparaiso, Limache, Serena, and Concepcion, and have sheltered thousands of unfortunates. In the epochs of epidemics these holy women have been most devoted, and during the late war many of them have labored in the army hospitals.

THE ARMY.

The regular army of the Republic, which never in times of peace exceeded 3,500 men, was reduced, at the beginning of the late war (1878), to the number of 2,700. Since the war began, no less than 60,000 have been enlisted. At present there are 22,000 men in the field, as follows:

In Lima and Northern Peru, .	15,000
In Cacna and Tarapaca, .	3,000
On the Araucanian frontier, . .	4,000

According to the register of 1881, the regular army was composed of 12,436 men, as follows:

10 Battalions of Infantry, with 9,040 men.
3 Regiments of Cavalry, " 1,296 "
2 " " Artillery, " 2,100 "

The National Guards, liable to be called into active service, in 1850 numbered 75,000 men, and might now number 100,000, but for economical reasons really only numbers 20,400. The Cavalry Militia was organized in 1876. The army was commanded in 1881 by 10 generals, 21 colonels, 77 lieutenant-colonels, 103 sergeant-majors, 191 captains, 181 lieutenants, 332 sub-lieutenants; total, 915—an increase over 1880 of 226 officers. At present the number is still greater. Including the arms and cannon recovered in the war from Peru, Chile possesses now more than 500 cannon, some of them of large caliber (1,000 pounds), and a 100,000 stand of arms. All her forts are well fortified, Valparaiso especially, since 1866–69.

NAVY.

The Chilean navy, which has attained equal renown with the army in the last war, has, besides two powerful war vessels being constructed in England, the *Artura Prat* and the *Esmerelda*, the following:

2 iron-clads—*Blanco, Encalado* and *Almirante Cochrane*.
1 monitor—*Huascar.*

2 corvettes—*O'Higgins* and *Chacabuco.*

2 cruisers—*Magallanes* and *Pilcomayo.*

4 steam transports — *Amazonas, Angamos, Abtao* and *Chile.*

2 frigates (sailing).

3 steam tugs, and various other small steamers.

11 torpedo boats, recently purchased, of a speed of twenty-two miles an hour.

The navy has 1,200 effective seamen, including the following officers :

1 vice-admiral.

4 rear-admirals.

11 captains of iron-clads.

10 captains of frigates.

22 captains of corvettes.

25 first lieutenants.

22 second lieutenants.

3 midshipmen.

39   "   not examined (*aspirantes*).

114 adjutants.

The Pacific coast of South America is favorable to navigation between Valparaiso and Guayaquil. Still magnetic variations little understood have occasioned many shipwrecks. The English Company has lost not less than twenty vessels since its beginning, in 1842; and Chile has recently (October 1881, and August, 1882) seen two of her transports, the *Payta* and the *Pisagua,* go down in Surco and Talaverry.

MERCANTILE MARINE.

The merchant marine of the Republic had been on the increase since the war with Spain in 1866. In 1879 it was composed of one hundred and six sailing vessels and thirty steamers. During the first year of the war there was a large decrease, but since then there has been a gradual increase. The coast trade has developed, and some of the Chilean vessels have even been called into the foreign carrying trade. The number of vessels May, 1880 and 1881, was as follows :

1880. 12 Steamers, 6 Tugs, 13 Barks, 2 Brigs, 4 Schooners, 12 Pilot Boats
1881. 12 Steamers, 6 Tugs, 2 Ships, 31 Barks, 3 Brigs, 5 Schooners 15. Pilot Boats.

There are five steamship companies doing business on the coast, one of them, the Pacific Steam Navigation Company, of England, having one of the largest fleets in the world. Its steamers sail bi-monthly to England, by way of the Straits of Magellan, and weekly to Panama. The South American Company, of Chile, runs a line of steamers as far north as Panama and as far south as Chiloe. The German Line, of Hamburg, runs to that port, and the French line, of Havre, to that port. The Lota Company employs several steamers in the coal and copper trade. The tug company of Valparaiso employs five or six small tug boats. The Spanish line belonging to the Marquis of Campo has just been inaugurated (September, 1882). All these companies represent a fleet of more than a hundred vessels, the United States not possessing a single one of them all. There is a Chilean Whaling Company, and several small fishing establishments. The most important one is ably managed by a Chilean seaman at Tumbes, near Talcahuano. Valparaiso Bay has two floating docks which serve for war vessels, steamers, and merchant vessels. At Talcahuano, the government is constructing new docks for the use of her ironclads, and expending several millions on them. In most of the ports are fixed or revolving light-houses, and in Santiago, there is a weather bureau which is of great service to navigation in general.

DIPLOMATIC SERVICE.

From the foundation to the late war Chile was very meagre in her diplomatic service, having only four foreign ministers,—one in Europe, one in the United States, and others in Peru and Bolivia; but now she has no less than twelve plenipotentiaries accredited to France, England, Germany, United States, Mexico, Central America, Columbia, Brazil,

Argentine Republic, Uruguay, Ecuador, and Peru. Her consular system is sufficiently extensive, but miserably remunerated. All the nations enumerated above have representatives resident in Chile. Spain and Russia have never yet acknowledged the independence of the republics formerly Spanish colonies. The difficulties with Spain, growing out of the war of 1865-66, are about to be adjusted. At the present moment a war vessel from that country is on its way for that purpose, and to re-establish commercial relations between the two countries. The diplomatic and consular service of the Republic in 1881 cost $102,105. To-day the cost is nearly double that, and if account be made for the difference of exchange, it will be treble that amount.

PUBLIC WORKS.

Chile has in operation 1,102 miles of railroad, and surveys are being made for the speedy construction of as much more; one line being intended to extend the central line, which runs from Valparaiso and Santiago to Angol, as far as Valdivia, thus traversing the territory of Araucania. This will do more to civilize the Indians than all the armies.

To Chile belongs the honor of constructing (1850) the first railroad in South America, that from Caldera to Copiapo. Her different railroads and highways are given in the following tables. *Railroads belonging to the State.* The railroad between Santiago and Valparaiso, with its branch from Las Vegas to Santa Rosa, in the Andes, is 144 miles long. The southern road, from Santiago to Talcahuano, is 359 miles, and to Angol 352 miles. The entire length, including the branch to Palmilla, is 446 miles. Total owned by the State, 590 miles. *Railroads belonging to companies,* excluding those of Tarapaca:—

Line from Mejillones to Cerro Gordo,	16 miles.
" " Antofogasta to Salinas de Dorado,	79 "
" " Taltal to the saltpetre mines of Cachiyu-yal,	60 "
" " Chanaral to Hundido,	55 "

Line from Caldera to Copiapo, with branches to
Puquios, San Antonio, and Chanarcillo, 101 miles.
"   "   Carrizal to Upper Carrizal and Cerro
Blanco,   74   "
"   "   Coquimbo to Serena, Tamaya and Ovalle, 62   "
"   "   Tongoy to Tamaya,   40   "
"   "   Laraquete to Quilanchanquin,   25   "

Total,   513 miles.

The State lines had cost for construction up to 1880 nearly
$40,000,000, obtained for the most part from British loans in
this form :—

The line from Santiago to Valparaiso, $12,925,334
"   "   "   the south,   26,028,575

During 1880 these roads transported 1,362,989 passengers
and 569,385 tons of cargo. The receipts were $2,142,985.

There are in operation in Chile 1,102 miles, besides the
short lines used in the coal mines of Coronel, Lota, Lebu, and
Punta Arenas. At Santiago and Valparaiso, and from
Old San Antonio to the mouth of the Maipo, there are street
railways, with a total length of 35 miles. In addition to these
there are over 700 public roads, kept in repair at government
expense, with a total length of 18,600 miles. There are also
1,600 mule paths, with a total length of 17,000 miles. These
are kept in repair by the municipalities, or private individuals,
or companies. There are, also, 78 navigable streams, with a
total navigable extent of 2,800 miles.

MAILS AND TELEGRAPHS.

The number of post-offices in 1880 was 335, and during
that year they handled 19,675,500 letters, papers, and pack-
ages. The department has also a postal money-order system.

The government owns a system of electric telegraph lines.
In the year just mentioned there were 102 offices with 178
instruments. The total length of wire, including some tempo-
rary lines used in the military operations at the north, was
5,700 miles. A new line has since been constructed to
Ancud, giving twelve additional offices and 473 miles. The

number of telegrams transmitted was 258,684, containing 5,990,525 words. There is a private line between Santiago and Valparaiso—the American line—and another between these two cities and Buenos Ayres, opened in 1872 and connecting with Europe. Altogether Chile has in operation more than 6,200 miles of wire. There is at present a bill before Congress to appropriate $400,000 to double these lines. Tacna and Ancud, the two extremes of these lines, are nearly 2,000 miles apart. There is a marine cable to Callao, and it has been completed to Panama, thus connecting with Mexico and the United States.

COMMERCE.

The commerce of the Republic is prosperous, and this country, by reason of its agricultural products for export and its extraordinary mineral riches, is one of the great markets of the world, although so small. The two following tables prepared by the Bureau of Statistics in 1882, relating to the commercial transactions of the Republic give the details:

Importation.—The importation of foreign goods to Chile in 1880 amounted to $29,716,004, as follows:

Articles of food,	$6,123,467
Textile fabrics,	8,319,791
Raw materials,	3,699,458
Clothing and jewelry,	1,926,843
Machines, instruments and hardware,	2,825,601
Household furniture,	1,459,589
Railroad and telegraph materials,	531,454
Wines and liquors,	559,735
Tobacco,	870,160
Gold, silver and copper metals,	19,336
Scientific instruments, art treasures, etc.,	373,380
Drugs, medicines, etc.,	304,200
Fire-arms and ammunition,	37,342
Miscellaneous,	2,636,521
Silver bullion,	13,152
Gold bullion,	16,275
Total,	$29,716,004

3

England is the largest importer, Germany and France come next, while the United States holds the fourth place. About the time of the independence (1817–1830) the United States sent more to Chile than did Great Britain. The nations which have imported the largest amounts are the following:

England,	$13,398,324
Germany,	4,785,642
France,	4,399,035
United States,	1,667,078
Argentine Republic,	1,465,063
Peru,	1,313,726
Spain,	603,028
Brazil,	521,657
Belgium,	484,497
Italy,	295,594

Exportation.—The articles and products which Chile exported, in 1880, amounted to $51,648,549, an increase over 1879 of $8,990,710. They were as follows:

Grain and produce,	$11,663,015
Metals,	37,811,150
Manufactured articles,	93,173
Miscellaneous.	109,093
Gold bullion,	57,265
Silver bullion,	1,185,867
Imported articles,	727,058

The agricultural products exported were:

Wheat,	138,777,700	$7,449,902
Flour,	11,419,000	1,003,952
Barley,	3,127,500	130,227
Wool,	2,207,100	507,904
Wines,	144,312 gallons,	122,594

The mineral exported products were:

Bar copper,	$13,912,641
Ingot copper,	1,431,314
Copper ores,	437,215
Stove coal,	404,872

The total imports and exports for this year amounted to $87,195,918, the imports being $35,075,246, and the exports, $52,120,672.

The trade between the various ports of the Republic was:

In 1879,	$35,618,119
In 1880,	53,558,637
Increase,	$17,940,118

The shipping with foreign countries showed the following number of vessels:

Entered—Sailing vessels,	689	with	418,176 tons
Steamers,	648	"	762,668 "
Cleared—Sailing vessels,	530	"	326,280 "
Steamers,	734	"	891,164 "

The coast trade showed in the same time:

Entered—Sailing vessels,	2,240	with	772,036 tons
Steamers,	2,423	"	2,067,650 "
Cleared—Sailing vessels,	2,362	"	842,528 "
Steamers,	2,287	"	1,924,694 "

Including the territories of Antofogasta and Tarapaca, which Chile occupied the entire shipping for the year ending March, 1881, was as follows:

	ENTERED.			CLEARED.		
Number of Ports.	Vessels.	Tons.	Passengers.	Vessels.	Tons.	Passengers.
34	6,153	2,279,212	37,711	6,204	4,205,337	27,171

According to the inaugural address delivered by President Santa Maria, June 1, 1882, before the National Congress, the exports amounted in 1881 to $60,519,827, and the imports to $39,341,351. The grand total of the commerce, including goods in transit, was $108,585,046. The export values, including guano and saltpetre from Tarapaca, were: Minerals, $47,145,757, being $9,333,667 more than 1880; agricultural products, $9,884,232, being $1,778,783 more than 1880; guano, $1,792,411; saltpetre, $22,891,786. The Government has just offered in the markets of Europe the sale of a million tons of guano from Tarapaca and Lobao Islands, and will share the proceeds with the lawful creditors and bondholders of Peru.

In Valparaiso the Government has very large bonded warehouses, which cost between three and four million dollars. They were intended to be fire-proof, but are proof against the fire-engine, as was recently shown by a destructive fire in one of them. For ten years past an iron wharf has been in process of construction. It is now approaching completion, and will cost two million dollars.

NATIONAL INDUSTRIES.

Mr. M. G. Carmona, the able chief of the office of statistics in Valparaiso, to whom, as well as to Mr. Asta-Burnaga, so well known in the United States, we owe the greater part of the statistics of this article, said in 1876 that agriculture and mining are the most important industries of the country. Some advancement has also been made in manufacture. There are manufactories of cloth, silks, paper, metal amalgamation, castings, oil, sugar refining, carriages, furniture, wool and hemp goods, ceramics, pottery, candles and soap, lumber sawing, lime and brick, whisky, wine and beer, steam boilers, leather, dyeing, marble cutting, and many other industries, and manual arts and trades.

Among the various agricultural and other products, we should mention, on account of their abundance, superior quality and commercial value, wheat, flour, barley, wool, hides, potatoes, bee honey, building lumber, hay and bran. There are exported also, in considerable quantities, house birds, salted beef, beeswax, dried beef, macaroni, beans, fruits, crackers, eggs, vegetables, linseed, corn, lard, butter, nuts and cheese. The native wines are very highly esteemed, and have a very large consumption in the country. This industry is becoming more important every day, and already sends to foreign countries millions of gallons annually. The following is a table of the principal agricultural products produced and exported.

	Produced.	Exported.
Peas,	24,749,077 pounds.	68,343 pounds.
Corn,	30,524,025 "	2,377,546 "
Wheat,	794,121,581 "	181,955,494 "
Flour,		58,426,264 "
Barley,	273,085,105 "	99,637,799 "
Wool,	10,243,860 "	3,757,518 "
Potatoes,	162,055,968 "	22,986,816 "
Nuts,	2,530,001 "	3,226,170 "
Beans,	45,793,607 "	3,217,986 "

In mining, Chile occupies a very high position among
the nations richest in minerals. Its territory contains very
rich deposits, in which are found every metal known. The
most important are copper, silver, stone coal, gold, cobalt,
nickel, lead, and mercury. There is also marble, porphyry,
lapis-lazuli, tin, borax, saltpetre, aluminium, agate, quartz,
granite, and other silicates, zinc, antimony, chalcedony, barytes,
magnesia, jasper, slate, lime, gypsum, argil, building stones, as
granite, grindlestone, and various others in the arts and industries. The exportations of the principal mineral products in
the years 1874 and 1875 were as follows :—

	1874.	1875.
Copper, in bars and ingots,	73,419,528 lbs.	78,287,486 lbs.
Copper regulus,	51,053,153 "	38,273,204 "
Silver in bars,	164,603 "	161,618 "
Copper and silver regulus,	8,635,690 "	6,302,802 "
Copper ores,	12,817,618 "	19,131,921 "
Silver regulus,	93,429 "	82,238 "
Stone coal,		578,600 "

Mineral exports from 1844 to 1875 :

	Value.
Copper in bars and ingots,	$155,077,806
Copper regulus, .	84,515,195
Silver in bars,	71,544,629
Copper ores,	33,553,903
Gold and silver coin,	21,263,964
Silver ores,	15,708,542

	Value.
Copper and silver regulus,	$13,189,958
Stone coal,	6,089,632
Gold bullion,	2,017,164

At the Continental Exhibition, held at Buenos Ayres (March to August, 1882), Chile, although having had only a month for preparation, competed with great honor to her natural productions and manufactures. She received seventeen medals of the first class, some of the second, and many bronze medals and honorable mentions, amounting in all to one hundred and seventeen premiums. The products which attracted the most attention in this international strife were her cloths, ropes, sugar, liquors, especially the wines, which are so superior and are receiving such incalculable advances.

The native timbers exhibited by the National Agricultural Society, one of the most beneficial institutions of the country, were represented by two hundred different kinds. The lumber of Chile is excellent. At the south there exists a species of wood, the *luma* of Chiloe, of the consistency of iron. In 1827 the government of France gave a contract for bringing Chilean timbers to her navy yards, and during the colonial days there were built in Talcahuano and Valparaiso no less than ten native-built vessels of ordinary size. But now the Chilean government buys all her war vessels in Europe, and only builds launches and flat-boats at the mouth of the Maule and other rivers. These launches are sent to Peru, and even to Ecuador, manned by only two men, and carrying generally cargoes of wood and lumber.

Chile must of necessity ultimately become an industrial nation like England, Switzerland, and the German provinces of the Rhine. The Argentine Republic, New Zealand, Austria and California are competing with the same agricultural products, and already usurp Chile's former supremacy. Foreign immigration and the completion of the transandine railroad, which is in process of construction from the other-side of the Andes, will contribute to the favorable solution of the matter.

NATURAL RESOURCES.

The most stable and healthy natural wealth of Chile is found in its agriculture. Mr. Cuadra, the present Secretary of the Treasury, estimated ten years ago that the value of real estate in Chile was $700,000,000. To-day, with the improvements introduced and the higher value of land, the total valuation should not be less than $1,000,000,000. No calculation can be made of the mineral wealth. The silver mines of Copiapo and Atacama are recovering their former richness; and the copper mines, although much reduced, still yield considerable quantities. A single one, the Pique mine at Tamaya, has yielded, in the last twenty years, $12,000,000. Lately (September, 1882) rich discoveries of silver have been made in the Cachinal Mountains near Taltal. The value of these new mines is estimated at hundreds of thousands and even millions of dollars. Recent discoveries of gold have also been made which evince the ancient wealth of this country in that metal for which it was so famous in the time of the incas. It has been calculated that in the eighteenth century, thanks to the cheapness of labor, Chile produced not less than thirty thousand pounds of gold, and in the time of Valdivia, from one mine alone, the Quilacoya, the Indians took out two hundred pounds a day. In 1881 some traces of this wealth were found in the ravines about Lebu, not far from the spot where that great captain was sacrificed. This confirms the opinion that no small part of the ransom of Atahualpa came from Chile. During this same year it is calculated that these ravines at Lebu yielded a half million dollars, notwithstanding the washings were operated under the old form of monopoly which the Spanish laws gave to the discoverer, and not in accordance with the system of free labor, personal reward, and licenses which have produced such prodigious results in California, New Zealand and Australia.

The circulating capital of Chile, as represented last year by the principal banks, was as follows:

BANKS.	Year of organization.	Nominal capital subscribed.	Capital paid in.	Available Capital.	
				Reserve fund.	Total.
Valparaiso,	1856	$20,500,000	$5,125,000	$600,000	$5,725,000
National,	1865	16,000,000	4,000,000	500,000	4,500,000
Alianza, Agricola,	1868	1,593,600	1,593,600	22,500	1,616,100
Concepcion,	1871	1,000,000	400,000	50,600	450,600
Consolidado, Mobiliario,	1870		1,125,000	70,000	1,195,000
Union,	1873	500,000	216,500	15,000	231,500
A. Edwards & Co.,	1867		1,500,000	250,000	1,750,000
Matte & Co.,	1875		1,000,000		1,000,000
Melipilla,	1878	60,000	60,000	3,200	63,200
Total, June 30, 1881.		$39,653,600	$15,020,100	$1,511,300	$16,531,400

The great private fortunes are as numerous in Chili, considering its extent and importance, as in the United States. The Edwards family possesses a fortune of thirty millions; the Cousino-Goyenechea family, owners of the coal mines of Lota, possesses a fortune of fifteen millions; the Matte and Brown families possess similar amounts. In February, 1882, there was published a list of seventy-eight Chilean millionaires, representing the sum of one hundred and eighty million dollars.

There are also numerous societies of credit, industries, mines, coal, etc. One of these, the Lota Coal Mining Company, has an annual net profit of nine hundred thousand dollars. There is also a loan association and a hypothecating bank, which have made loans of many millions to the land owners and renters. Recently life insurance companies have begun to do business here. The Equitable Company of New York stands at the head by its honesty, amount of its capital, and number of its policies.

NATIONAL REVENUES.

The national revenues have increased extraordinarily. During the time of the colony, when the public expenses did not exceed $300,000, they were entirely provided for by annual appropriations made by the Viceroy of Peru for the support of the army. The total expenses in 1776, under Governor Jauregui, were $295,277. In 1810, at the time of the emancipation, the revenues had reached $400,000. With free trade, development of agriculture, mining and other industries, the income quintupled during the last ten years of the war for independence (1816–26). The estimate that year, under President Freire, was $1,736,823. In 1836, under President Prieto, the revenues had augmented to $2,321,936; ten years later, in 1846, under President Bulnes, to $3,741,672; and in the next decade, under President Montt (1856), to $5,708,058. Since that epoch, on account of the introduction of railroads, the institution of banks (1855), the introduction of paper money (1878), the development of coal mining on a large scale, and the cheapening of blasting materials for mines, the incomes have doubled every ten years, as follows:

Administration of President		Perez, 1866,	$9,079,936
"	"	Errazuris, 1878,	16,830,000
"	"	Santa Maria, 1882,	39,008,219

PUBLIC EXPENSES.

A century ago the expenses of the government, indicating the state of advancement of the various services, are represented by the following figures, given by President Amat:

Government service, .	$4,596
Custom Houses, .	9,460
Interior,	9,500
War,	198,278
Courts,	31,465
Church (not including tithes),	320
Treasury,	49,714
Total,	$295,277

Sixty years later, in 1836, the expenses had reached the following:

Home and foreign service, .	$328,251
Interior department,	776,409
Army and navy,	939,542
Total,	$1,990,202

In 1881 they had reached the following:

Interior,		$4,699,581.39
Foreign relations,	$101,515	
Colonization,	180,536	
		282,051.00
Courts,	$658,545.22	
Church,	237,030.00	
Education,	1,119,620.44	
		2,015,195.66
Treasury,		7,613,963.63
Army,	$1,314,585.44	
National Guards,	·299,508.78	
		1,614,094.22
Navy,		2,299,676.64
Total,		$18,524,562.54

PUBLIC DEBT.

The home and foreign debt of Chile, according to careful statistics, prepared in the government offices, to June 1, 1882, was as follows:

Foreign debt (gold 48 pence to the dollar),	$34,870,000.00
Home debt (gold 35 pence to the dollar, the present rate of exchange),	56,546,384.85
Total,	$91,416,384.85

HISTORY.

Governor Don Diego de Almagro, discontented with the portion of the treasures of Peru which fell to his lot in the distribution made by his famous comrade Don Francisco Pizarro, resolved to advance to the discovery and conquest of Chile, which was already famous for its abundance of gold. The name, Chile, according to some, is derived from *chiri*, from *chuchua* (cold), from the snows on the mountains which the Peruvians had to cross; and, according to others, from the name of the *cacique* of Aconcagua, in the time of the Spanish invasion.

The incas had conquered the country, as far south as the Maule River, a century before, and had established a kind of valley confederation. They had manufactories of pottery and coarse fabrics at Melipilla, Talagante, and the Mapocho River, the ruins of which are yet visible. They worked the rich gold mines and washings, which, according to Rosalis, paid the inca at Cuzco an annual tribute of 14½ *arrobas* of gold (312½ pounds). They marked the ingots with the breasts of a woman.

The incas erected temples to the sun in Quillota, Colina, and other places; introduced the *llama* as a beast of burden, and opened canals, as that of Salto, which still irrigates the plain of Santiago. The dominion of the incas, by rights, extended to the Maule. They defended with great firmness the valley of the Mapocho, with forces summoned from Callipiumo, in Paine pass, to the south of the Cachapoal, which proves that really their dominion only extended to the northern bank of this river.

It is curious that *Chilli* means *cold* in Quichua and the same (chilly) in English; and also that the first Spaniard to penetrate into the interior was not Almagro, but a soldier named Pedro Calvo Barrientos, whose ears had been cut off in Cuzco for some crime, and who came to hide his dishonor in the valley of the Aconcagua, to whose *caciques* he taught the art of war. Almagro did not get any farther than Aconcagua and Melipilla, where he found a little gold. His captain, Gomez de Alvarado, having notified him that the rivers to the south, in such a hard winter (1536), would be found impassable, and the frontiers of the ferocious Promauca Indians who lived from the Cachapoal to the Bio-Bio, defended, he returned to Cuzco by way of the desert of Atacama, Tarapaca and Arequipa, meeting with great hardships. He was beheaded by his ungrateful rivals in 1538.

Captain Pedro de Valdivia, who was more youthful and vigorous, asked permission of Pizarro to go and settle Chile in his name. Leaving Cuzco with a hundred and forty soldiers, in October, 1540, he founded Santiago, February 12, 1541. This great explorer traversed the whole country,

and subdued it as far as the city of Valdivia. He took
away large quantities of gold, which soon attracted a numerous immigration. He founded Serena, Valparaiso, Concepcion,
and seven cities in Araucania, which were then the principal
ones of Chile. Their ruins still exist, and are being repeopled
slowly by the Chileans, as Angol, Imperial, Villa Rica and
Arauco. But the Araucanian Indians—brave, indomitable,
and excellent horsemen, like the Apaches of New Mexico—
revolted, and killed Valdivia near this last-named city, on
Christmas Eve, 1553. From this date the decadence of the
colony began.

During the reign of Philip III. several illustrious captains,
such as Garcia Ramon (1600) and Alfonso de Rivera (1612),
came from Spain, and succeeded in somewhat allaying the
eternal rebellion of these savages, who, during the first century
of the conquest, cost Spain a hundred thousand lives and
eighty million ducats.

During the seventeenth century there were several notable
administrators and warriors, among them Fernandez de Cor-
dova (1625), Lazo de la Vega (1629), the Marquis of Baides
(1646), and, especially, Don Juan Henriques, who governed
in the time of Charles II. (1670). Under the government of
his successor, Jose de Garro, called "the Holy" because of
his probity and disinterestedness, the kingdom was afflicted
by an invasion of buccaneers (1680-85), and having been
before greatly injured by the earthquake of 1647, the previous
wars, pestilence, and droughts, it was now determined to relin-
quish it; so it was totally abandoned to its ancient barbarous
possessors. The seventeenth century was the dark age for the
colony.

It is worthy of observation, that, among the Spanish pos-
sessions of the new world, Chile and New Grenada alone
received the name of "kingdom." Peru, the Plate, and even
Mexico, were only vice-royalties.

During the eighteenth century several important fran-
chises were granted to commerce, and the richness of the gold
mines attracted a strong current of economical working-people
from Biscay; and, with this labor and honesty, the colony gained

great prosperity. Presidents Manso, Amat, O'Higgins and Jauregui,—all of whom were afterwards viceroys of Peru,— distinguished themselves among its captains-general as able administrators. It is owing to the energy which the riches and prosperity produced in the colonial aristocracy, that Chile raised, in conjunction with Buenos Ayres, Caracas and Bogota, the cry of independence, and named its first President and Governing Assembly September 18, 1810. There followed an unsettled and discordant period called the "Old Country," in which the viceroy of Peru, Abascal, was permitted to govern the country again. His successor, Pesuela, sent an army to subdue the country, which, under the command of General Ossorio, overthrew the patriot forces at Rancagua October 2, 1814. But San Martin, governor of Mendoza, with the remnant of the Chilean army, which had fled across the Andes, and the generous assistance of Buenos Ayres, formed a division of four thousand men, and making use of seven thousand mules and three thousand horses,' he crossed the Andes of Aconcagua, as Hannibal had crossed the Alps, in January, 1817, and completely overthrew the Spaniards in the battles of Chacabuco (February 12,1817) and Maipo (April 5, 1818). This era has been called the "New Country." General O'Higgins was named dictator February 16, 1817, and accomplished the independence of Peru, San Martin advancing to Lima with the united armies of Chile and La Plata, July 21, 1821. He declared the independence of Peru the 28th of the same month. He had been powerfully assisted by the Chilean squadron, commanded by the famous Lord Cochrane and the young admiral Blanco Encalada. But after San Martin had left, and O'Higgins had been superseded, by a popular movement, January 28, 1823, there followed a series of political fluctuations and trials caused chiefly by Presidents Freire, Pinto, and Vicuna, until the liberal or *pipiolos* administration was overthrown by the old conservative or *pelucones* party of O'Higgins, under the command of General Prieto and his counsellor, Diego Portales, in the bloody battle of Lircai, April 17, 1830.

Prieto, the victorious general, was named constitutional

president, for the defense of the conservative constitution, which was promulgated May 25, 1833. Portales was made his Prime Minister. He had been simply a merchant in Santiago and Lima, but succeeded in governing the country until Peru was in war a second time in 1836. This powerful minister was murdered in a mutiny of the expeditionary troops (June 6, 1837). Chile continued the war under the command of General Bulnes, who had been one of the chief founders of the Republic. He was always victorious, and overthrew the Peru-Bolivian confederation, destroying its army under Santa Cruz in the celebrated battle of Yungai (January 20, 1839).

Through this means the political parties of Chile were reconciled and the victorious general was elected president. And from that time an epoch of aggrandizement and prosperity began for Chile. For fifty years this prosperity has had but brief interruptions (1851 and 1859) caused by political controversies and bad passions at election times. In great contrast with all the other republics of the Spanish race, the presidents, Prieto, Bulnes, Montt and Perez each ruled for the constitutional period of ten years. During the term of the last-named, the war between Spain and Peru (1865–66) took place. Chile generously rushed to the defense of Peru, and spent uselessly $30,000,000, and allowed its principal port to be bombarded rather than dishonor her flag before the Spanish Government and Admiral Mendez Nunez.

The Constitution of 1833 was reformed by the liberal Congresses which sat during the administration of President Perez. The term of the presidential office was limited to five years. Then followed President Federico Errazuris, who began the great public works, and armed the country 1871–76; and Anibal Pinto, whose administration is chiefly notable for the war into which the country was drawn in 1879 (and which still continues) in consequence of a secret treaty against her, made between Peru and Bolivia in 1873, but not discovered until seven years later.

In this long war Chile has only received victory, prestige and riches, which have placed it along with the Argentine Republic at the head of all the nations of like origin.

The port of Antofagasta was occupied February 14, 1879, and some Bolivian skirmishers dispersed in a slight engagement at Calama on the banks of the Loa, on the 23d of the following March. A maritime war was begun, but was without decisive results until the capture of the famous Peruvian monitor Huascar before Angamos Point, October 8 of the same year. The ocean thus freed from the enemy's vessels, ten thousand Chilean soldiers were landed at Pisagua, a port of Tarapaca, November 2, 1879, and in the battle of San Francisco one-half of this force overthrew the allied Peruvian and Bolivian army of eleven thousand men. From that day Chile has remained in peaceful possession of all this rich and desirable territory as far as the Camarones River. After these victories the operations of the army were retarded by vain hopes of peace, and it became necessary to undertake a second campaign against the provinces of Moquehua and Tacna, which resulted in the bloody battle of Tacna, in which the allies were again defeated May 26, 1880. Twenty thousand combatants were engaged on the two sides.

The port of Arica was taken by assault at the point of the bayonet, the 7th of the following June; and although it would have been an easy and opportune undertaking to carry the victory into unarmed and panic-stricken Lima, new negotiations of peace were entered upon which delayed the result, and protracted the definitive campaign through eight months more. At the end of December, 1880, 25,000 Chileans set sail in three divisions from Arica. They occupied the valley of the Lurin strategically to the end of this month. They then undertook the assault of the formidable works, which were defended by 30,000 men and 200 cannon, and protected Lima. The 17th of January, 1881, they victoriously entered that capital for the third time during the century, after having totally annihilated both the army and the squadron on the previous days, the 13th and 15th, in the celebrated battles of San Juan, Chorillos, and Miraflores,—the most bloody and greatest that have ever taken place in South America.

The three campaigns of Antofagasta, Tacna, and Lima, which brought about ten combats and battles, besides several other encounters and blockades, cost the army and navy of Chile 10,000 men in killed and wounded, without counting the considerable number of sick and disabled, caused by the unhealthy climate of Peru.

The cost of the war has been $30,000,000, not counting the indirect losses, which have, perhaps, been twice as much. These losses, and the total extinction of the military power of Peru, should have produced immediate peace after the decisive battles which took place at Lima. But a generous and equivocal policy on the part of Chile, and the unreasonable and unwarranted interference on the part of Secretary Blaine, of the United States, which effected, by means of his agents, Hurlbut in Lima, and Adams in La Paz, have caused the war to be indefinitely prolonged, thus imposing heavy expenses of money and life on Chile, without bettering, in the least, the defenders, who are spending their last strength in desperation, and without causing the least manifestation of inability on the part of the victor to maintain her interests, her future, and her security, and, much less, to accept the forced intervention of any neutral power, European or American.

B. V. M.

www.ingramcontent.com/pod-product-compliance
Lightning Source LLC
Chambersburg PA
CBHW032123080426
42733CB00008B/1038